How to Draw
Faces

This book is dedicated to Jesse.

Published in the United States of America by The Child's World®
PO Box 326 • Chanhassen, MN 55317-0326
800-599-READ • www.childsworld.com

Acknowledgments
Design and Production: The Creative Spark, San Juan Capistrano, CA
Series Editor: Elizabeth Sirimarco Budd
Illustration: Rob Court

Library of Congress Cataloging-in-Publication Data
Court, Rob, 1956–
  How to draw faces / by Rob Court.
      p. cm. — (The Scribbles Institute)
  Includes index.
  ISBN 1-59296-151-7 (library bound : alk. paper)
  1. Face in art. 2. Drawing—Technique. I. Title.
  NC770.C68 2004
  743.4'2—dc22
                                        2004005319

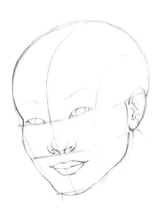

How to Draw
Faces

Rob Court

It is not enough to believe what you see,
you must also understand what you see.

—Leonardo da Vinci

Parents and Teachers,

Children love to draw! It is an essential part of a child's learning process. Drawing skills are used to investigate both natural and constructed environments, record observations, solve problems, and express ideas. The purpose of this book is to help students advance through the challenges of drawing and to encourage the use of drawing in school projects. The reader is also introduced to the elements of visual art—lines, shapes, patterns, form, texture, light, space, and color—and their importance in the fundamentals of drawing.

The Scribbles Institute is devoted to educational materials that keep creativity in our schools and in our children's dreams. Our mission is to empower young creative thinkers with knowledge in visual art while helping to improve their drawing skills. Students, parents, and teachers are invited to visit our Web site—www.scribblesinstitute.com—for useful information and guidance. You can even get advice from a drawing coach!

Contents

Drawing Faces Is Fun!

You can draw your friends in art class or your family at home. You can draw the face of someone famous while looking at a photograph. Or you can draw the face of a superhero from your imagination.

The easy steps in this book will help you draw faces for school projects or for fun. Find a big piece of paper and a pencil. You can get started right now!

Forming the Head and Face
Underneath the skin and muscles of the head is the skull. Knowing its form helps artists draw faces that look real. Shown below is the side view of a hard, bony skull. See how it forms the **profile** of a woman's face on page 7.

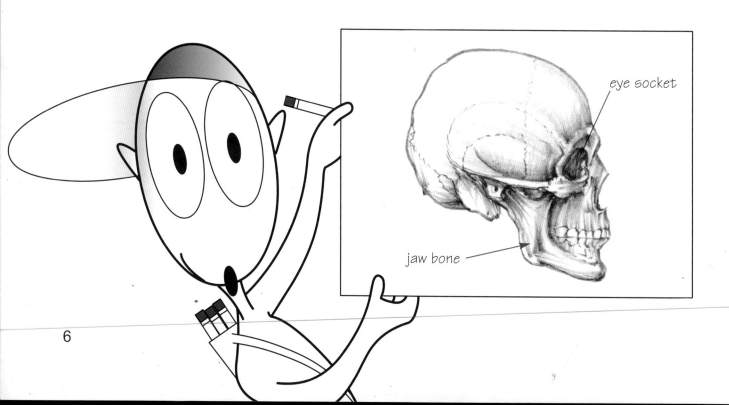

eye socket

jaw bone

Using Guidelines

Artists lightly sketch guidelines to show the shape of a face. **Horizontal** and **vertical** guidelines help to place features such as the eyes, nose, mouth, and ears.

guideline

vertical guideline

horizontal guideline

Proportions

In the drawing below, guidelines and features divide the head. The drawing shows a young woman's profile. Her features form the **proportions** of her face. Notice that the measurement from the eye guideline (or eyeline) to the top of her head is the same as from the eyeline to her chin.

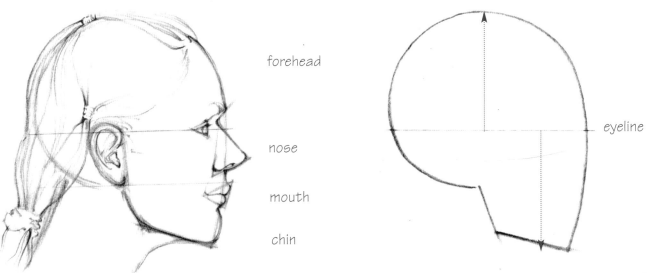

forehead

nose

mouth

chin

eyeline

Drawing with Shapes

Drawing the profile of a young woman is easy when you start with basic shapes. Sketch these shapes lightly. This way, you can erase them later as you finish your picture.

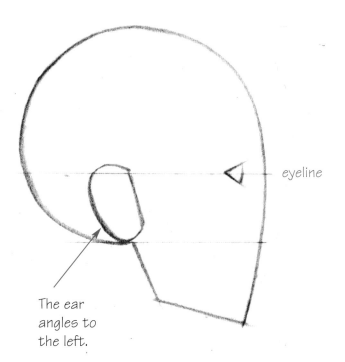

eyeline

The ear angles to the left.

Young Woman

1 Start by sketching the shape for the head. Divide it in half by drawing the eyeline. Draw another horizontal guideline, halfway between the eyeline and chin. Next, draw the shape for the eye. The back of the eye touches the eyeline. Draw the shape for the ear. Notice how it rises above the eyeline.

2 Sketch the shapes for the nose and mouth. Notice how the top of the mouth touches the guideline. Draw the inside of the ear. Compare your drawing with the one at right. Do you like the shape of the head? Are the eye and nose where you want them? Make changes if you need to.

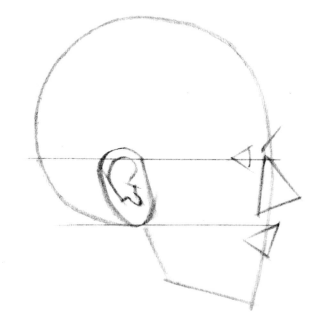

Drawing with Lines

Drawing **outlines** around the edge of the shapes forms the woman's profile. Keep drawing until you like the outline. Remember to draw lightly so that you can erase if you need to.

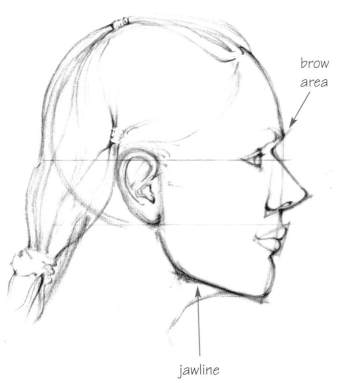

brow area

jawline

3 Carefully sketch an outline for the nose. Notice the slant of the nose and where it connects to the brow area. Continue by drawing a curved line for the nose. Add curved lines to make the eyebrow. Next, draw the outlines for the mouth. Notice the curve of the chin and how the jawline turns toward the ear. Continue with details such as the eyelid and eyelashes. Draw curved lines for the inside of the ear. Add lines for the neck. Sketch guidelines for hair.

4 Using angled and curved lines, draw a darker outline to finish your picture. Notice the curved lines that show the roundness of the eye and the edges of her lips. Add final lines to show waves in her hair.

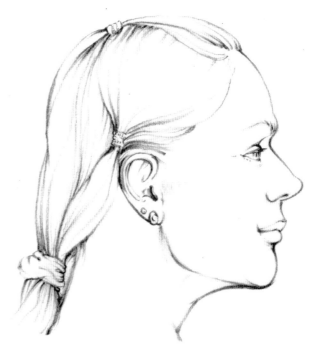

Everyone's face is different. The features of a man's face are different from those of a woman's face. Start with basic shapes, then draw a man's profile.

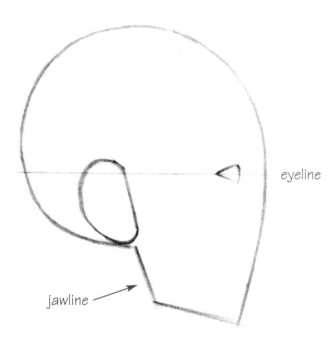

eyeline

jawline

Young Man

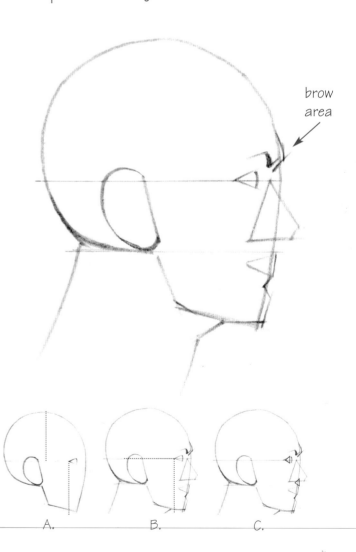

1 Start by sketching the shape of the head. Divide it in half by drawing the eyeline. Draw another guideline, halfway between the eyeline and chin. Next, draw the shapes for the eye and ear.

brow area

2 Sketch the shapes for the nose and mouth. Then draw the eyebrow. Begin sketching lines to form the brow area and chin. Add lines for the neck.

HOT TIP ## Check Proportions

A. The distance from the eyeline to the top of the head is the same as from the eyeline to the chin.

B. The distance from the eyeline to chin is the same as from the back of the eye to the back of the ear.

C. The distance from the bottom of the nose to the mouth is equal to the height of the eye.

A.   B.   C.

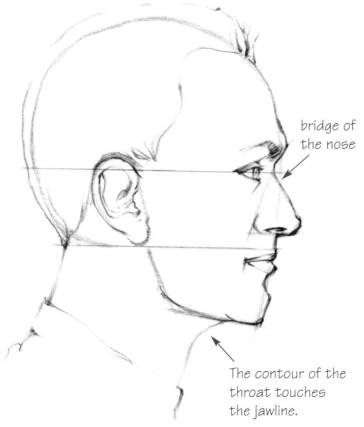

bridge of
the nose

The contour of the
throat touches
the jawline.

3 After checking proportions, continue by drawing **contour** lines for the face. Carefully sketch the brow area, the bridge of the nose, and the chin. Draw curved lines for the nose and eyebrow. Continue with details such as the eyelid and eyelashes. Next, draw the outlines for the mouth, including a short line at the corner of the mouth. Pay attention to the contours inside the ear. Add lines for the neck and hair.

4 To finish your picture, draw darker contour lines to form the profile of the man. Notice the contour lines that form the nose and how it attaches to the face. See how the contour lines form the eyelids. Be sure to add eyelashes. Finish drawing the ear. Add lines to show the hair.

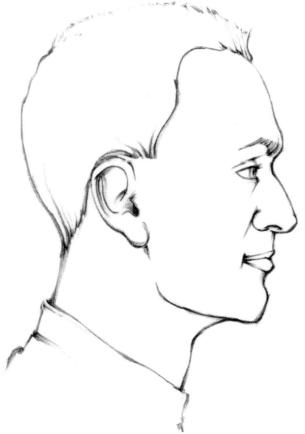

The face changes shape as the head turns toward you. Use horizontal and vertical guidelines to show the proportions of a front view of a man's face.

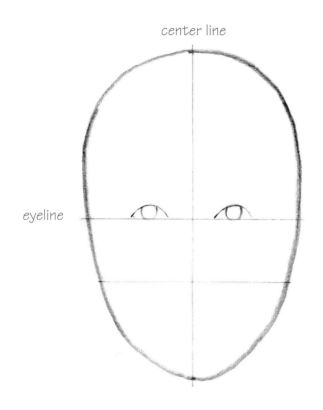

center line

eyeline

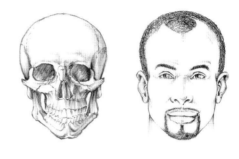

Front View of a Man

1 Lightly sketch the shape for the head. Divide it in half by drawing the center line. Next, draw the eyeline. Draw another guideline halfway between the eyeline and chin. Sketch the shapes for the eyes and curved lines for the eyelids. See how they touch the eyeline.

2 Continue by drawing curved lines to complete the eyes. Lightly sketch a circle for the tip of the nose. Then sketch curved lines to form the nostrils. Notice how they touch the guideline. Next, sketch the shapes for the ears and mouth.

 The width of the face is about five eyes across.

The bottom of the lip is about halfway between the nose and the tip of the chin.

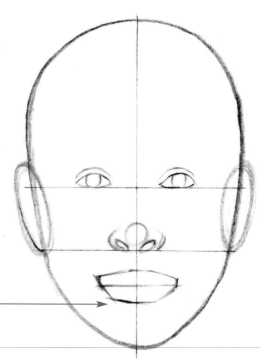

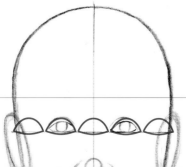

12

3 Begin drawing the contour lines. Sketch lightly so you can make changes. Draw the curves of the cheeks and jaw. Next, draw curved lines to form the ears. Notice where the rim of the ear connects to the side of the head. Carefully sketch lines to form the eyes. Notice the lines of the eye sockets that show underneath the skin. Add lines for the hair, beard, and neck.

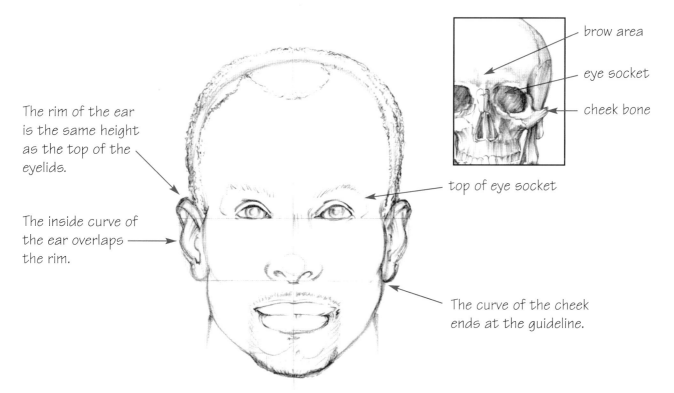

brow area

eye socket

cheek bone

The rim of the ear is the same height as the top of the eyelids.

top of eye socket

The inside curve of the ear overlaps the rim.

The curve of the cheek ends at the guideline.

4 With a darker pencil, draw contour lines to finish the man's face. Include details such as the ears and round eyes. Contour lines form the nose. Darken the openings for the nostrils. Then lightly draw lines to show where the nose attaches to the brow area. Notice how lines show the roundness of the lips. Use heavier, darker lines to finish the hair, eyebrows, and beard.

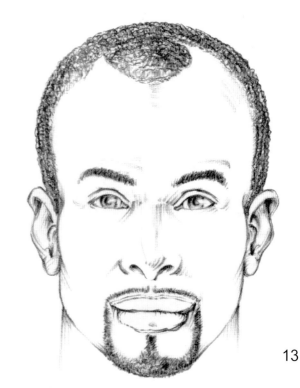

Faces in Art

Artists use different ways of drawing to create faces. The drawing style shown below uses flowing, curved lines to make a woman's face. Her long hair and facial features are drawn with simple lines.

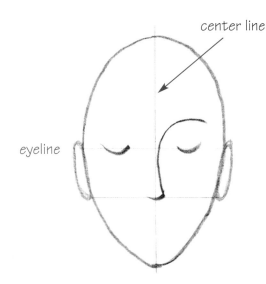

center line

eyeline

1 Start by sketching the shape for the head. Draw the center line and eyeline. Then draw the guideline for the bottom of the nose and ears. Sketch the curved line for the eyebrow and nose. Add curved lines for closed eyes and the ears.

2 Continue by sketching lines for the lips. Draw two short lines for the corners of the mouth. Add the other eyebrow. Sketch long, flowing lines for hair.

The neck twists slightly as her face turns toward you.

Curved lines show waves of hair overlapping each other.

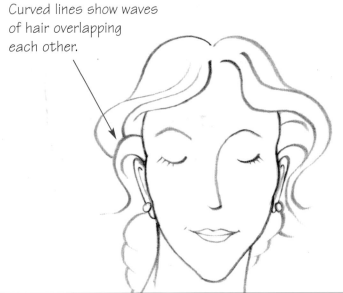

3 Darken the contour lines to finish the woman's face. Draw lighter, curved lines to show strands of hair. Add details such as earrings and eyelashes.

Anime is a style of drawing used by cartoonists in Japan. Large eyes and angled lines for hair are often used in Anime drawings. How are this woman's facial features different from those of the woman on page 14?

1 Sketch the shape for the head. Notice the proportions of the wide forehead and small chin. Next, draw the center line and eyeline. Then draw the shapes for the eyes, nose, mouth, and ears.

center line

eyeline

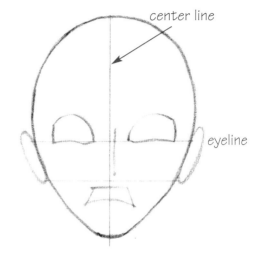

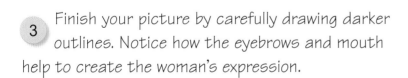

2 Continue by sketching long, angled lines for the hair. See how the pointed strands hang over the eye. Add lines for the neck and large jacket collar.

3 Finish your picture by carefully drawing darker outlines. Notice how the eyebrows and mouth help to create the woman's expression.

When drawing faces, let the facial features express what the character is thinking or feeling.

Artists use sketches to plan finished paintings. Sketched lines form this girl's hat, called a beret, as well as her hair and her clothing. Notice where the artist spent more time drawing the features of her face, especially the details of her eyes.

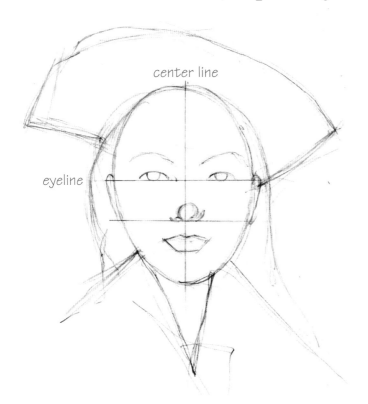

Girl with Beret

1 Sketch the shape of the girl's face. Divide it in half with the center line. Draw the eyeline and guideline for the bottom of the nose. Sketch shapes for the eyes, nose, mouth, and ears. Lightly sketch the lines showing the beret, hair, neck, and shoulders.

2 Continue by sketching darker lines to show the girl's cheeks, chin, and neck. Carefully sketched lines form the eyes, lips, and nose. Keep sketching lines to form the beret and hair.

[HOT TIP] Easy Measurements

The distances from the outside corner of the right eye, to the outside corner of the left eye, to the edge of the bottom lip are the same.

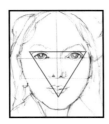

3 Continue sketching the girl's facial features, beret, hair, and clothing. Dark lines are used to show the roundness of the eyes. Notice how corrections are drawn on top of other lines, instead of erasing them.

Lightly sketched lines show the bridge of the nose.

contours of cheek

corrections drawn over guidelines

How the surface of something feels is called texture. Use lines to show the texture of clothing and hair.

Copying other artists helps you to learn about drawing. This drawing was copied after *Girl with Beret* by Camille Corot (1796–1875). Corot lived in France and was an important painter.

Form

With practice, you can change flat shapes into three-dimensional or "3-D" form. The three-quarter view of an Iroquois man's head is formed by showing both the front and side of his face.

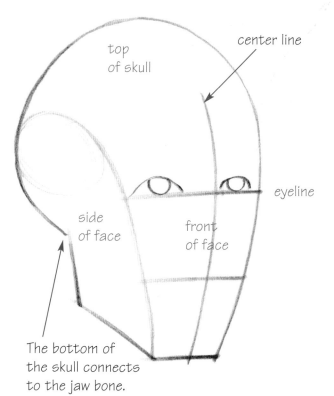

top of skull

center line

eyeline

side of face

front of face

The bottom of the skull connects to the jaw bone.

Three-Quarter View of an Iroquois

1 Sketch the basic form of the head. Notice how a circle forms the round skull. Draw the center line to follow the curve of the forehead. Draw the eyeline across the width of the front of the face. It continues, at an angle, on the side of the face, stopping at the back of the head. Place the eyes on the eyeline. Next, draw the guideline for the nose on the front and side of the face. It is the same angle as the eyeline.

2 Next, lightly sketch guidelines to form the brow area. Sketch lines to form the cheek and chin. Then sketch the shape for the nose. See how the bridge connects to the brow. Draw the shapes for the mouth and ear. Add guidelines for hair and the neck.

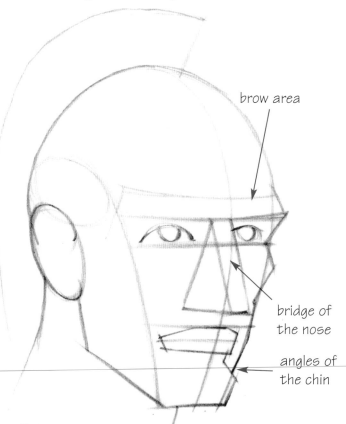

brow area

bridge of the nose

angles of the chin

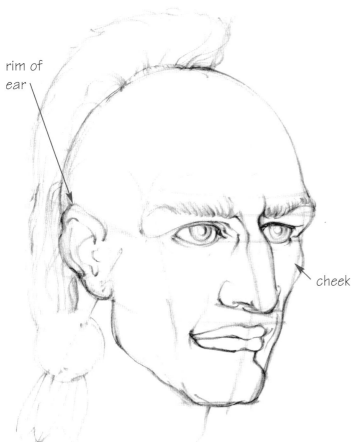

rim of
ear

cheek

3 Take a moment to look at your drawing. Is the top of the skull large enough? Is the brow area wider than the chin? Continue by sketching contour lines to form the nose and brow area. Look carefully at the shape of the eyebrows. Draw curved lines to show the roundness of the eyes. Notice how the nose hides part of the eye. Notice how the cheeks are drawn on both sides of the face.

4 Carefully draw the darker contour lines to finish your drawing. Add details such as the texture of the hair and feathers. Use the side of your pencil lead to draw soft lines for wrinkles on the forehead.

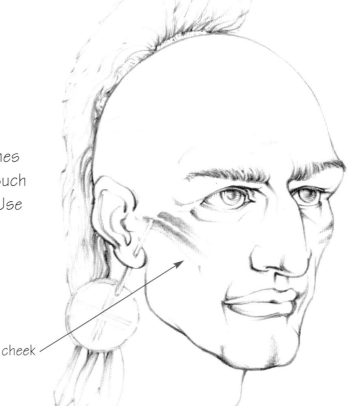

cheek

Light and Shadows

By using light and dark **tones,** you can create shadows.
Drawing shadows helps you see the form of a girl's face.

center line

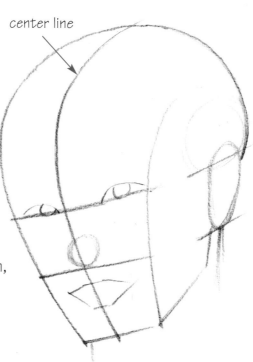

Light Source

Places where light comes from are called light sources. The sun is a light source. A lamp is also a light source. In the drawing below, a light source shines on a sphere. How do the shadows change as the light changes position?

Asian Girl

1 Sketch the form of the head. Draw the center line and eyeline to show the tilt of the head. Place the eyes, nose, mouth, and ears as shown. Add lines to make the neck.

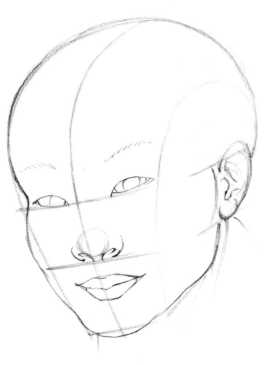

2 Carefully outline the head and features of the face. Add lines for eyebrows and where you'll place the hair. Compare the girl's facial features to the Iroquois man on page 19. The man's lips are shaped differently. How are the eyes, nose, and cheeks different? Press lightly with your pencil when drawing your outlines. This makes it easier to erase the shapes before drawing the shadows shown in step 4.

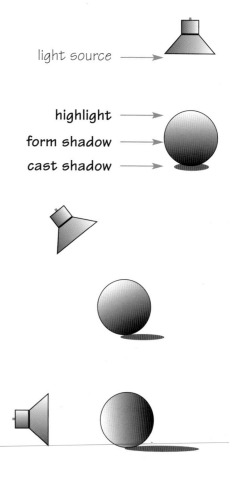

light source

highlight
form shadow
cast shadow

3 Before adding shadows, carefully draw darker outlines that form the face, hair, and clothing. Draw contour lines to show round cheeks and clothing folds. See the smooth curves of the nose and lips. Darken the nostrils. Add lines to show her hair. Continue until you like what you've drawn. Then carefully erase your guidelines.

4 Start drawing shadows in areas where no light shines from the light source. Hold your pencil on its side, press firmly, and begin drawing the darkest shadows on the neck and hair. Shadows are lighter where more light touches. Lighten the pressure on your pencil as you draw lighter shadows. Fade the shadows away to the white of the paper where there are highlights. Notice the softness of the shading on the cheeks, brow area, and nose. Reflections make highlights in the eyes.

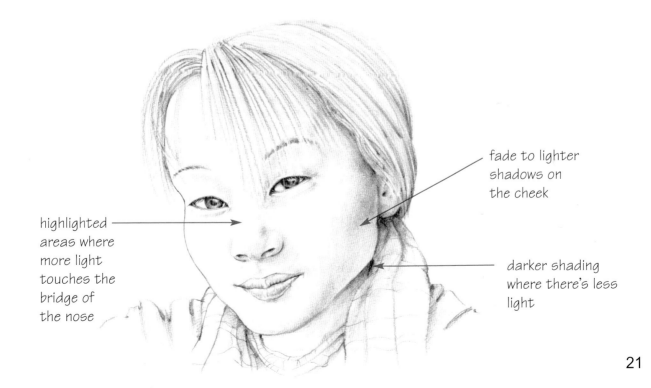

highlighted areas where more light touches the bridge of the nose

fade to lighter shadows on the cheek

darker shading where there's less light

The Portrait

When you draw features to look like someone's face, it is called a portrait. By carefully drawing his features, you can create a portrait of basketball player Michael Jordan.

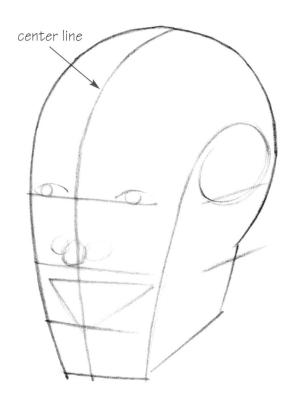

center line

Michael Jordan

1 Sketch the form of the head. Draw the center line and eyeline. Next, draw guidelines to place the eyes, nose, and ears. Add the shape for his big smile.

When drawing Michael Jordan, carefully sketch features that people will recognize. Concentrate on the form of his head, cheeks, and eyes. Take time to draw his friendly smile.

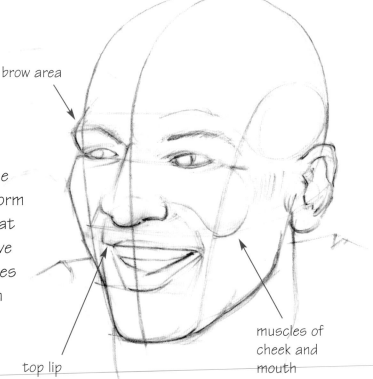

brow area

muscles of cheek and mouth

top lip

2 Sketch the outlines of the head, facial features, and neck. Draw a very light line for the teeth. Next, lightly sketch lines to form the ear. Compare your picture with the one at right. Make changes until you like what you've drawn. Notice the lines used to place muscles for the cheeks and mouth. Press lightly with your pencil when drawing your lines.

3 Before adding shadows, carefully draw contour lines that form the facial features, hair, and clothing. Draw contour lines to show round cheeks and clothing folds. See the smooth curves of the nose and lips. Darken the nostrils and eyebrows. Continue until you like what you've drawn. Then carefully erase your guidelines.

HOT TIP ## Blending Shadows

To show the smooth texture of skin, you can lighten shadows by blending. Start drawing shadows in areas where no light shines from the light source. Hold your pencil on its side, press firmly, and begin drawing the darkest shadows on the neck. To blend, gently rub the shadows with your fingertip. Fade the shadows away to the white of the paper where there are highlights. Erase areas where there are highlights. Notice the softness of the shading on the cheeks, brow area, and nose. Use light grey tones for the teeth, instead of outlines.

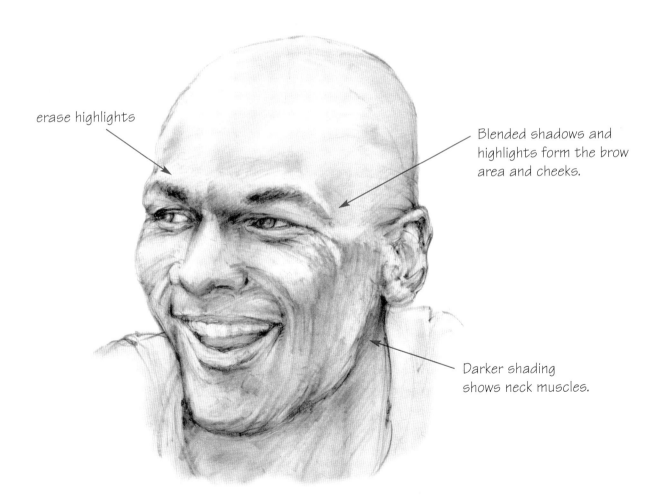

erase highlights

Blended shadows and highlights form the brow area and cheeks.

Darker shading shows neck muscles.

Abraham Lincoln was the sixteenth president of the United States. The profile of his face is famous. Begin drawing his portrait by drawing the shape of his head.

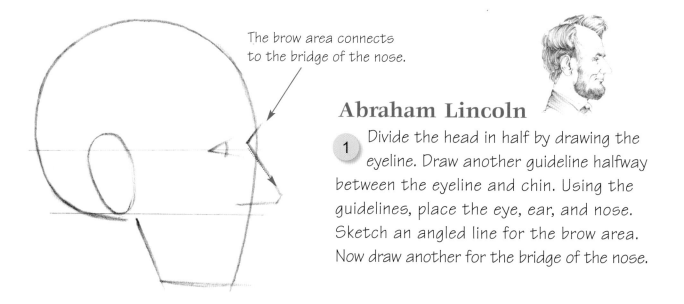

The brow area connects to the bridge of the nose.

Abraham Lincoln

1 Divide the head in half by drawing the eyeline. Draw another guideline halfway between the eyeline and chin. Using the guidelines, place the eye, ear, and nose. Sketch an angled line for the brow area. Now draw another for the bridge of the nose.

2 Continue by sketching the contour line for the outside edge of the nose, lips, and chin. Notice the direction of the jawline as it curves toward the ear. Next, start sketching the lines for the rim and inside shapes of the ear. Then carefully draw curved lines for the eye and eyelid. Lightly draw the eyebrow and muscles near the nose and corner of the mouth. Add two lines for the neck.

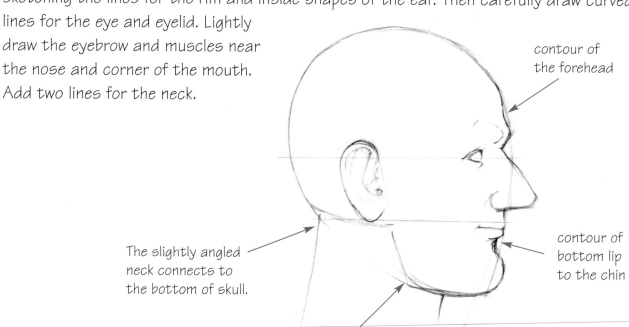

contour of the forehead

contour of bottom lip to the chin

The slightly angled neck connects to the bottom of skull.

jawline

3 When you start adding features such as the hair, eyebrows, and beard, it begins to look like Abraham Lincoln. Notice how the hair flows in different directions. Begin sketching darker contour lines for the facial features. Pay close attention to the brow, nose, and chin. Carefully draw the contours of the eye and ear. Add outlines for the clothing. Start blending the shadows for the cheek, corners of the mouth, and the wrinkles on the forehead.

4 Use a darker pencil to draw the thick, dark hair. (Turn to page 27 to learn more about pencils.) To create the hair, turn your pencil on its side and use heavy strokes where the shadows are darkest. Lighten the pressure on your pencil as it moves toward the highlights. To create highlights, erase contrasting lines in the hair. Pay close attention to the direction the hair flows as you make your strokes. Shorter, thinner pencil strokes are used to make the beard.

highlight

darkest shadows

The Self-Portrait

When you draw a picture of yourself, it is called a self-portrait. Sit in front of a large mirror. You should be able to see your whole face and neck. Sit so you can move your arm freely while drawing. A drawing board or tablet will give you a sturdy surface on which to draw. Try to hold a pose while drawing for 20 minutes. Take a break and look at your drawing. Then pose for another 20 minutes to finish your self-portrait.

1 Pose in front of a light-colored wall or background. This makes it easier to see the form of your head. Start by sketching the shape of your face and hair. Pay attention to the outside edges of your face as you sketch. Use guidelines to divide the proportions and place facial features.

Take a break, if needed.

2 Continue by drawing the darker contour lines of the facial features, hair, and neck. Take time to draw details around the eyes and mouth. Lightly shade the bridge of the nose, cheeks, and brow area. It takes practice to draw portraits that look real. Just have patience, have fun, and concentrate!

Which Pencil Should You Use?

A standard "2B" or "2SOFT"' pencil works well for most drawings, but other pencils can make your drawing even more interesting.

Pencils are numbered according to how hard or soft the lead is. You'll find this number written on the pencil. A number combined with the letter "H" means the lead is hard (2H, 3H, 4H, etc.). When you draw with hard leads, the larger the number you use, the lighter and thinner your lines will be.

A number combined with the letter "B" means the lead is soft (2B, 4B, 6B, etc.). The lines you draw will get darker and thicker with larger numbers. Sometimes you will read "2SOFT" or "2B" on standard pencils used for schoolwork. When you see the letter "F" on a pencil, it means the pencil is of medium hardness.

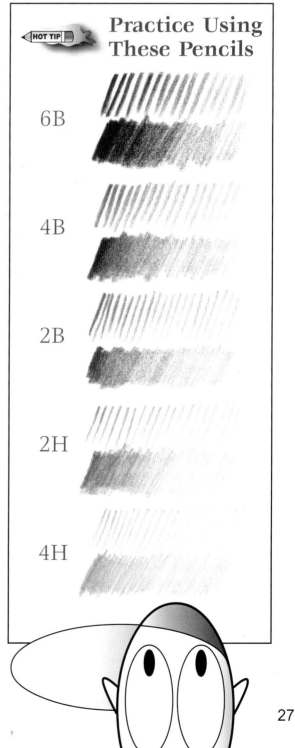

HOT TIP

Practice Using These Pencils

6B

4B

2B

2H

4H

Drawing with Color

By using colored pencils, you can make a drawing of a superhero more exciting. Create the colors of his face and costume by mixing yellow, blue, red, and black.

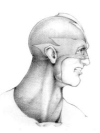

Superhero

1 Start by sketching the shape of the head. Draw the eyeline and guideline for the nose. Then draw the shape for the eye and ear. Add two lines for the neck. His jaw is tilted downward.

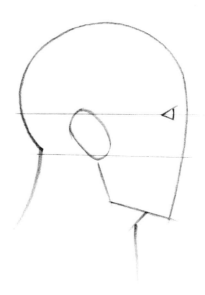

brow area of
face mask

2 Look at the picture to the left. Sketch the angled lines for the mouth and jaw. Continue by sketching the facial features and parts of his face mask. Lightly sketch the curved lines of the neck. Add guidelines for the shoulders.

neck muscle

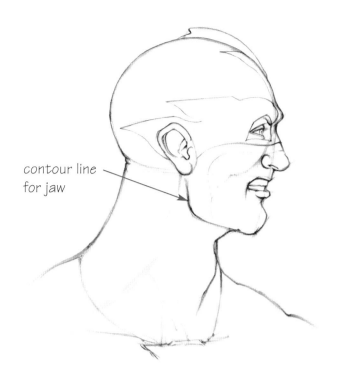

contour line
for jaw

3 Continue by carefully drawing darker contour lines for his facial features. Include details such as the eyelid and the ear. Darken details of the face mask. Draw contour lines for the clothing and the mask.

When you like the lines you've drawn, carefully erase all guidelines and prepare to add color.

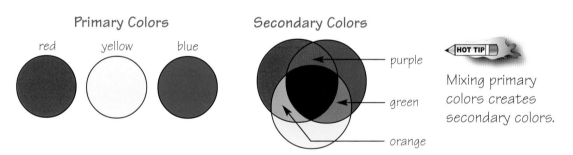

Primary Colors

red   yellow   blue

Secondary Colors

purple

green

orange

HOT TIP

Mixing primary colors creates secondary colors.

Adding one color on top of another while drawing is called layering. To learn how to layer primary colors, try using only yellow, blue, red, as well as black, in this drawing.

4 Lightly shade the areas of the face, including the eye and ear, with a yellow pencil. Think about the direction from where the light source is shining. Apply more pressure to darken areas where there are shadows. Darken areas around the cheek muscle, inside the ear, and around the eye. Add yellow to parts of the face mask and clothing.

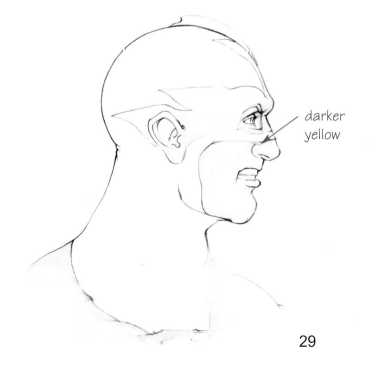

darker yellow

29

Mixing Colored Pencils Is Fun!

 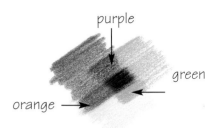

red

blue

yellow

purple

orange →

green

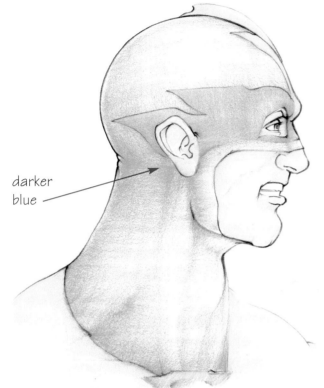

darker
blue

5 Next, add a layer of light blue over areas of the face mask. Where there are shadows, such as under the chin and around neck muscles, make the blue darker. Notice where the shading is darker to show the roundness of the skull. Mix a layer of blue on top of the yellow clothing.

What color do you get when you mix blue with yellow? Continue by mixing darker blue in shaded areas of the clothing.

6 Fun things start to happen when you add red to this illustration. Lightly shade the face with red. Continue until you get a flesh color you like. Add a layer of light red on the face mask. What color do you get when you add red on top of yellow areas? Make darker shadows around the muscles of the cheek, jaw, and neck. Add a little red to the lips, leaving white areas for highlights.

Shading with black creates the 3-D form of the muscles, face mask, and clothing. Notice the cast shadow around the jaw and inside the ear.

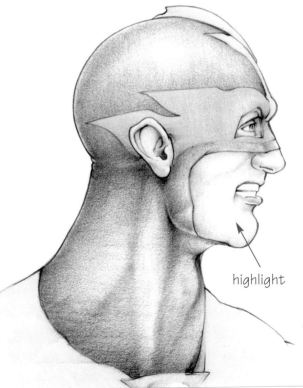

highlight

The Artist's Studio

Artists need a special place where they can relax and concentrate on their work.

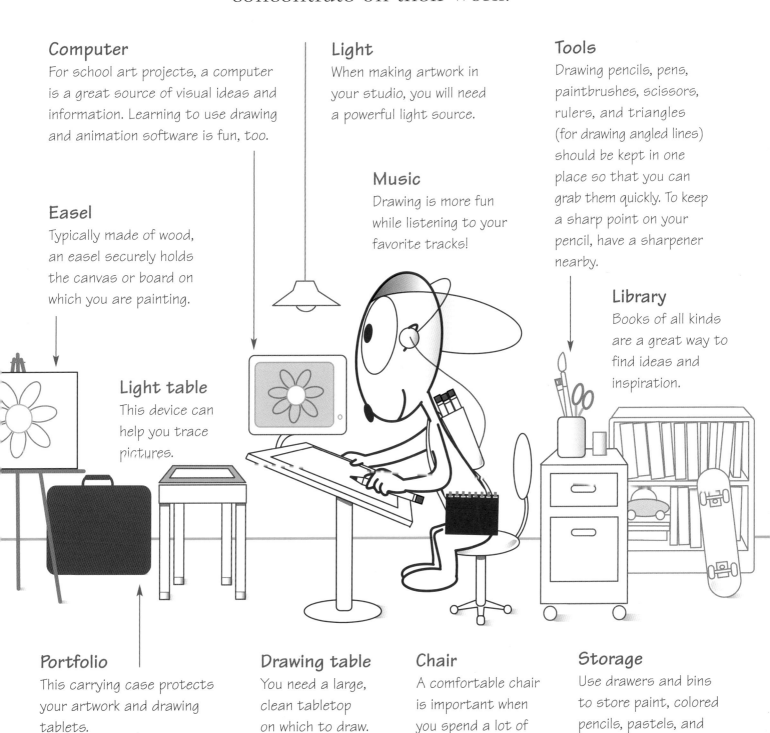

Computer
For school art projects, a computer is a great source of visual ideas and information. Learning to use drawing and animation software is fun, too.

Easel
Typically made of wood, an easel securely holds the canvas or board on which you are painting.

Light table
This device can help you trace pictures.

Light
When making artwork in your studio, you will need a powerful light source.

Music
Drawing is more fun while listening to your favorite tracks!

Tools
Drawing pencils, pens, paintbrushes, scissors, rulers, and triangles (for drawing angled lines) should be kept in one place so that you can grab them quickly. To keep a sharp point on your pencil, have a sharpener nearby.

Library
Books of all kinds are a great way to find ideas and inspiration.

Portfolio
This carrying case protects your artwork and drawing tablets.

Drawing table
You need a large, clean tabletop on which to draw.

Chair
A comfortable chair is important when you spend a lot of time drawing.

Storage
Use drawers and bins to store paint, colored pencils, pastels, and other supplies.

Glossary

A **cast shadow** is the shadow that a person, animal, or object throws on the ground, a wall, or other feature.

A **contour** is the outline of something; in your drawings, a contour line follows the natural shape of a person's face.

A **form shadow** is a shadow in a drawing that shows the form or shape of a person, animal, or object.

A **highlight** is the area or areas in a drawing that receive the most light from the light source.

A **horizontal** line moves from side to side; a person lying down is in a horizontal position.

Outlines are lines that show the shape of an object, animal, or person.

A **profile** is the side view of a person's face.

Proportions are the relations of two or more things in terms of their size; if something is in proportion, all its parts are in proper relation to each other.

Tones are lighter and darker shades of a color.

A **vertical** line is drawn straight up and down; a person standing up is in a vertical position.

Index

About the Author

Rob Court is a designer and illustrator. He started the Scribbles Institute™ to help people learn about the importance of drawing and visual art.